Stay Safe!

Bicycle Safety

Sue Barraclough

Heinemann Library
Chicago, Illinois

© 2008 Heinemann Library
a division of Reed Elsevier Inc.
Chicago, Illinois

Customer Service 888-454-2279
Visit our website at www.heinemannraintree.com

Illustrated by Paula Knight
Designed by Joanna Hinton-Malivoire
Picture research by Erica Martin
Printed and bound in China by South China Printing Co. Ltd.
12 11 10 09 08
10 9 8 7 6 5 4 3 2 1

ISBN 10-digit: 1-4034-9857-1 (hc) 1-4034-9864-4 (pb)

The Library of Congress has cataloged the first edition of this book as follows:
Barraclough, Sue.
  Bicycle safety / Sue Barraclough.
     p. cm. -- (Stay safe)
  Includes bibliographical references and index.
  ISBN-13: 978-1-4034-9857-1 (hc)
  ISBN-13: 978-1-4034-9864-9 (pb)
 1. Cycling--Safety measures--Juvenile literature. 2. Bicycles--Safety measures--Juvenile literature. I. Title.
  GV1055.B37 2008
  796.6028'9--dc22

                              2007016489

The paper used to print this books comes from sustainable resources.

Contents

Riding a bicycle is fun.

Do you know how to stay safe
on a bicycle?

Never ride a bicycle without
a helmet.

Always make sure your helmet fits you.

Never wear loose clothes on a bicycle.

Always wear clothes that fit well.
Always wear clothes that are bright.

Never ride a bicycle that is too big.

Always make sure you can touch
the ground.

Never go too fast.

12

Always check your brakes.

Never ride without your hands.

Always be seen and heard.

Never ride on busy roads.

Always ride on a safe path.

Never bike across a busy road.

Always use a crosswalk.

Always remember these safety rules.

Always stay safe on your bicycle.

Bicycle Safety Rules

- Make sure your helmet fits you.
- Wear clothes that fit well.
- Wear clothes that are bright.
- Make sure your feet can touch the ground.
- Ask a grown-up to check your brakes.
- Always be seen and heard.
- Ride on sidewalks or bike paths.
- Use crosswalks to cross busy roads.
- Get off and walk when you cross a road.

Picture Glossary

brake the part of a bicycle that makes it slow down or stop

crosswalk a place on the road where it is safe to cross. Crosswalks have special marks or lights.

helmet a special hard hat that protects your head

path an area next to roads that is set aside for people. A bike path is for people on bicycles.

Index

Note for Parents and Teachers

Books in this series teach children basic safety tips for common situations they may face. Ask children if they ride bikes. Discuss with them the importance of learning how to ride a bike safely and using proper equipment, such as helmets. Ask children to study the illustrations in the book and think about whether the behavior shown is safe or dangerous. You can ask the class to think of other bike safety rules and create a list for the class.

The text has been chosen with the advice of a literacy expert to ensure beginning readers success when reading independently or with moderate support.

You can support children's nonfiction literacy skills by helping students use the table of contents, picture glossary, and index.